Also by Peter O'Leary

POETRY
The Sampo
Phosphorescence of Thought
Luminous Epinoia
Depth Theology
Watchfulness

PROSE
Thick and Dazzling Darkness: Religious Poetry in a Secular Age
Gnostic Contagion: Robert Duncan & the Poetry of Illness

AS EDITOR
Ronald Johnson
Collected Later Poems
The Book of the Green Man
ARK
Radi os
The Shrubberies
To Do As Adam Did: Selected Poems

John Taggart
Is Music: Selected Poems

EARTH IS BEST

STUDIES FOR THE
ADVANCEMENT OF
THE SACRO-MAGICAL
SCIENCES NO. 1

Earth Is Best

PETER O'LEARY

THE CULTURAL SOCIETY : BROOKLYN : MMXIX

FOR PAM REHM

ELF OF PLANTS

Say on, sayers of the earth!
Delve! mould! pile the substantial words of the earth!

—WHITMAN

Erthe toc of erthe erthe wyth woh,
Erthe other erthe to the erthe droh,
Erthe leyde erthe in erthen throh,
Tho hevede erthe of erthe erthe ynoh.

—FROM A FOURTEENTH-CENTURY
ASH WEDNESDAY LITURGY

TO THE PUBLIC

After three years' labors to make light from the phosphorescence of thought, and after the struggle then to argue, to weave, and to compose a cosmology, and after an ordeal of divination (a kind of psychic crisis in which it became clear that there is no difference between acute anxiety and euphoria), I once again display my systems to the public.

Pattern recognition may have been the earliest discernment of the human creature. Here, once again, an elaborate pattern, premised on meaningful coincidences drawn from the dynamos of living forms, forms living outside the mind but discerned, in a kind of bewilderment, in our mind.

The Ancients entrusted their love to their Writing, to the full. I do too: My trust is in numen, lumen. A fire not imaginable? No. The soul-bright earth, cobwebbed with life. Soil's incessant neurology.

Rather than monotony, rather than the complacencies of lyric subjectivity, rather than the political economies of language, I have chosen to express these patterns in a poetry whose modes are theogony and mycology. The mind flourishes in poetry or withers in a prison of cant. Poetry is a *referential openness* unto the depths of the earth and into a conversation with its living forms, a complete coded protest against the powers of worldly dominion, a messianic predication of meanings, and a puzzlement.

EARTH IS BEST

FIRST AMANITA ODE

Pictured Rocks National Lakeshore, Upper Peninsula, Michigan

Earth is best, while asurian fire colors day and
night is silvery white, the radiance
divinity intensifies
in the tawny speckled
head

crowning from the duff of white pines
and birch trees flocked under
streaming slants of ante-vernal sun. Superior
detonations sound under lapis wind-tossed
flashes. In ancient times,

a lordly wealth of amanitas. Bellowing with power
in North Country orange. *Vesture-of-grand-
occasion*, Himalayan

priests intoned. True nature. Shining through.
Even in the closing season. A freakish
lutre to the fruits.

Autumn's pneumative semioclasm
exploding waves in limestone—bright choir
of illuminating sunlight. Shadow.
Shadow dreaming men. Metamorphoses of
vital gloom excrescent

mushrooms body forth as form—hundreds
of fly agarics in a Michigan
pine woods. *Move forward—what stirred? Move
backward*—the all-ceaseless pauses, woven repletion
of the scene, the pattern a clarion,
a sound and a call unanswered except in vocation—.

Creation is the task energy
in darkness undertakes where lurks an ante-solar sun
the onset of whose odor signals
Earth's unseen reticulations unspooling into
an everpresent antiquarian:

loam's rich undying gloom.

SECOND AMANITA ODE

Coils in a silo in cavernous open space downward sloping
lined with aluminum panels crosshatched with grids; a hum.
A droning range. Tuned to the key of E. And a glare of light.
Intensifying a holy living form in the nave of the silo.
No secret for the poet-priests. What is it? Wondrous. Wall
of light: like the enormous gills of a salamander. Like a reef.
Like a colossal bone-white fungus with a feathered flesh.
Like the central nervous system of some vast exposure the light
nurses from loam and shadow. Metamorphoses of gloom.
Phase-shifting flanging of sound. A woven texture reticulated.
It is forty arborescent feet tall with three polyporous
conch-like shelves. Stained with bioluminescent signatures.
Sutures of daylight. And a central spinal stalk vivid in the form.
There's a cord with bulbous contours out from which the life
of the animal emerges.
                        Seeing it. Consumed with knowledge of it
incoherent unconfirmed. Terrified. But I recognize this creature.
I am its expert. I walk on one of its tremoring shelves tilting
to move toward the column to touch it. What stirs?

Shadow's fruits are forms to shape out from the quarreling earth
the mind's devoured worth, soil's mash of relation
flexing hyphal threads repulsing with awareness enmesh.

THIRD AMANITA ODE

Moon and gloomy-star,   silver wheel,   blue lure
masker, toy : magic disk and doubt disk.
Wide-dark.   Cloudy wind-dark.   Twin-lit moistener.
Metal cloud-storm.   Loss beacon.   Night courser.
Orange summoner.   Strange radiator.   Scalpal-harasser.

Mushroom   food-jewel and madness-jewel.   Moon's stone and
Sun's bane.   Heaven's fiery backside.   Earth's threads, Earth's filters.
Resounder of the word's way   Moon's urine   mainstay pillar fulcrum
Monarch of everything that sees the Sun's light dazzling daytime mesh reseen
as a structured fiber of moonlight
waves rich in honey.
Pressed one.
Studs on the cudgel.

Forest   System of energy.   Green heliotroph.   Earth-vestiture.   Earth.
Mycelium manifestor. Animal laboratory. Light sieve. Light filter.
Moon fog. Mind fog. What the antipodal night drains through.
Detonation cushion.   Dense master.   Darkness thickener.

Shadow-bellower fire-wick. Silvery-white constellator.
Metaphor of living forms. Massive laws. Earth-vestiture of verdure.
Green shudder. Mountains mantle.
Birch or pine or hemlock.
Fir. Gallop of horses the winds
sound. Thou hast clothed thyself in sun-bursts
where the shadows in thee have thrived.

Books   Legendarium.   Demense.   Mountain fastness.

It seemed that a shadow hung over the fly agaric,
an ancestral curse; yes, a talon.

Olympic summits. Heights above the tree line.
Ample ursine foragers. Angelic consummators.
Cloaks of light, oil of light drizzled in my beard.
Sprinkled manifestations of the locomotion.
Walking and sauntering. The witness
of nearly constant walking.

The energies manifest the innumerable names of God.
Earth. Aurosis. *Luminous beams attune our speculation.*
Extended tendrils in the earth dusk. Hectares of fungi,
meshwork of minute shrouds. Nosochthonic toxicity mycelia neutralize.

Mycelial auscultation: attunement to the world through its mushrooms.

Eophanic harvest argenteous light tilts crisply in on.
Esculent morel: Moor with a conical cap. Honeycomb pattern
rough and delicious. Aurulent spume: gush of morning light
filtered through the trees: elm and ash, maple and oak. Rank
of morning nothing. Mushrooms hidden in plain sight. Brain
of fronds the oaks' bases grow. *Immortal Principle. Lord
of the Secret Way.* Light is the fluid in angelic dynamolosis.
Exalm crushed in Earth's shadow, its dusk
undulations. In the distance, then suddenly near, the alpine
warbler sounds its bracing call. *Vocation is everywhere.*
Communion is the volition of every living form.

::

A storm is a system of energy.
A storm is a manifestation of a system of energy.
A tree is a system of energy.

A mycelium is a long-branching, filamentously structured system of energy.

Energy is the economy of the mycelium, summoning living forms
hidden in the thoroughgoing ecology—beech and ash and
oak, in the mosquito's whining in the slowly warming morning,
shadows the lemon-yellow prothonotary bursts from
into the slash of sunlight the river surface ripples into.

Fathom ye hymnic chasms mycoremediation inundates:
As a species, humans
are adept at inventing toxins
but inept at removing them from our systems.
God put us on Earth to process toxins mushrooms degrade.
It's what we should do.

FIFTH AMANITA ODE

Soma's acrodromous doxeme.   I will
revive the gods with herbs. Necromancers. Evasive
answers from the necromancers. Milking rain
from the living cloud. Shook morning dew.
Who wove the loam with gloom.
Spores of an archaeon. Born in felt.

A megalithic holy element.   Tree ears.
Crazy with asceticism.   Mounting the wind.
Long-haired ascetics swathed in wind.
Mycelial filaments flaked in sand.

We have drunk the Soma
We have become immortal
We have gone to the light
We have found
the gods. What can hatred and malice of a mortal do to us now, O Immortal
    One.

Moon god   *whose pock-marked face*
                whose white flesh
                whose white rotundity before it breaks through the white veil
                whose crescent appears when the cap is bisected
                whose fruit is the night's.

Mushroom's beast-headed forming of energy—
outcroppings of oyster bunches
    brown buds, tips on small white shafts.
Matrix of spent coffee: substrate of spores.
Slow-motion gush of the fungal fruit
hibernal corona of infant oysters
fogged attentions manifest—
acrodromous doxeme of the gloom.

    Shadow crown   winter crown
    fronds of pored umber
loam alluminor.

Moon's snowstorm's static patterns.

::

ache
hear
care

::

Golden-shafted pentagram a dozen
flickers wing the shape of in strident
fading calls: aura
of April bluebirds.

::

Radium of daylight.
Mushroom: the point of wisdom, the primordial point.
Mushroom: the kingdom, the presence, the earthly queen.

SEVENTH AMANITA ODE

PINDARIAN DIRGE

Living forms thread even densest earth
hidden hollows ghost forms throng in
go beneath.

Being alive is already an end.
A god's tellic secrets
soil unburies

only in the eyes of one who sees:
God makes the archaeon. Hidden things
make all ends.

The huge Centaur, inspired. Cryptic keys
turn the bolts unlocking the sanctuaries
where love and destiny are stored.
Lord Sun! Even gods
won't fuck in daylight.

EIGHTH AMANITA ODE

MAY SONG

Woods: deep-zoned envisioner—thou
who knowest the end supreme of all things and everything
that leads there: the atmospheric pressures, the witnesses
of the turning worlds, the earth's tilth, what
makes us. You pantotelic muse—how's this?

In the mycelial penetralium, dendroiac frettings
at the peripheries sunbreaks highlight   and the shadows
mark the ground beneath which intermesh   hyphal holons
from which push   trillium's Maytime ally
deeply pitted   waxy   lustrous
yellow and esculent—

the cognitive pause, the moment's vernal settlement
the element attends. Springtime.

NINTH AMANITA ODE

Ob-Ugrian shudders, shamanistic numerousness
duskless summer days multiply
with intoxication. "Woman, bring me in
my three sun-dried fly agarics!"   Little people
whose realm the urine drinkers enter   flaunting
Siberian strength   piss
impregnated with berry juice and
an amanita's psychoactivation.   Raised spirits,
brisk, courageous, cheerful.   Tremors.

Merriness and melancholia.   Hidden little people you'll
imitate.   And macropsia.

"A small hole appearing to you
as a great pit, and a spoonful of water

as a lake."

TENTH AMANITA ODE

Creation in any form is praise even
from death's sweet devouring, even the Earth's
fruiting bodies coming forth from death—ascomycetic
spores—smooth, hyaline—puffed
on cool spring air. In a bewildering
variety of habitats.

ELEVENTH AMANITA ODE

ESCULENT WIND

And the waves of the air over the grasses
And the creak of the leaning tree against the tree standing
And the swallow flowing into the gust
And the wood ducks in the flooded field
And the vicious demonstrations of the blackbird
And the systematic expansion of what the eye can see
And the esculent honeycomb of light
And its waxy multiplications

THE DOGS

for Lissa Wolsak

———————————————————————————————————

Blood-gushered mountainside a brass parapegma of noon
glares behind: gore of hides. Beasts all slain. Shadeless midday. Specterless
differentiation. Glad day zodiacs augur. Awl of insight; hunters'
blades. Actaeon: and the spirits of motion. Actaeon
uttering:

> *::invisible solar stellatum : blue daytime::*
> *::chalcedony, hyacinth, opal, sapphire, slate::*
> *::Crystal. Ash. Hyacinth.::*

> "Lads. We've had luck our nets and spears
> are dripping with. Fortune's thirst for blood quenched.
> The chariot's an auroral throne dawn radiates from,
> a furnace of ruby ore noon roars out from. We're done.
> We'll kill again tomorrow, tracking boar through these
> trackless wastes. Let's go home and roast these hams."

Actaeon's men. Dragging together the nets to bind them. Ceasing.

A valley there. Dense with pine. With cypress. Called Gargaphie.
Diana's holy retreat. In whose hidden Arcanum a grotto.
Creased green with shade. No hand could have made it.
But Nature makes art—imitating herself. An arch of living rock.
Soft tufa. Effervescing source. On the left. A stream—
waving, lucid—sounding out. And pooling. Where
spears of grasses natter. Here's where the virgin of the wild
woods bathes. Crystal waters. Green shade. One nymph
holds her hunting spear. Holds her epic bow. One nymph takes
her robe. And two nymphs unbind the sandals from her feet.
And one Theban nymph whose fingers are nimblest quickly knots
Diana's unbraided hair streaming in the swishing cooler air. Of the grove.
Other nymphs bring the urns. Steaming with water. Let's call them:
Wooly Milk Cap. And Velvet Stem. And Elm Oyster. And Slippery Jill. And
    Black Trumpet.
And Titania bathes. She's splendid. Completely. Unlike any other being.
But Cadmus's scion—Actaeon. There he is. His senses relaxing. Dilating.
Stepping uncertainly. In woods he doesn't know. Entering that holy grove.
Fate's firebrand his torch. Flare in the vernal shadow. He's *there*. They see him.

Furious percussions on the air. As they thrum their breastbones.
Helicoptering sound. Arms in shocking, sudden motion. All of them
ululating. Shrill pitch sirening atop woofered chopping.
They're all nude. Quick—they try to cover Diana with their bodies.
But she's immense. A towering beauty. Like Dawn's incoming redness.

Like sunlight's silver-tipped spears. Like a new unanticipated thought.
Changing your life forever. She radiates. At him. Everlasting. Eternity's
involuntary taste. It shocks him. She's unarmed and can't kill him.
Water: she flicks it at him instead. Sprinkles him with wicked doom.
Look at me. Sound of several octaves. Sounded at once. A deity's fantastic
  vocalizing.
Tell someone. What you've seen. I dare you. In his skull's proteins: the water's
tendrils root their curse. Actaeon's head—it aches. A migraine's lightning
actualized as antlers. Stag's horns. His jawbone narrows, extends. Fingers
harden into hoofs; hands densify, tighten. His arms—slender legs.
His legs—tremble with a frightened gait, awakened.
His body—a maculate, velvety hide. At last she adds
to his heart startled fear. At that, he rips through the woods.
So nimble! So fast. Time vanishes. In his freedom.
A shimmering pool. Vision of his rack of horns. "Misery!" A word as
  animalian moan.
Weeping. Lachrymose tantrum of his unchanged mind. Its shames. Flowing
  into form.
His form—charging on in fear. Impeded. Timorous. Running.

Dogs. Hexagons of sunlight they shatter in their mad dash.
Dogs. His fucking dogs. On the run. First comes Blackfoot,
an elegant Spartan deerhound, lunging in strides his anatomy's
hippodrome urges; and next courses Helltrail whuffing like a
Cretan mare. Velocity's roar. Humming aura of lurches and panting.
Next, the Arcadians: Born of Thunder; Faux Pax; and Torrent.

Elf-Slayer. Dart. Rioter. Shog. Deadly Galerina. Wood Rot. Fumerol.
Like a fresh gush of thought, like a havoc of inspiration: Earthstar, Death
    Liquor.
Demon Tiger. Demon Dragon. Shrill-tongued Hylactor. Swift Horror.
Rudiment. Dynamite. Kindler and his sister Acid. Ash. And more.
The whole pack. Turbid. Lusting for blood. Pouring over rocks. Over
cliffs. Over hard ways scents should vanish from. After *him*! His best dogs.

His pleas to his dogs: a stag's braying. They charge
eagerly after. Actaeon submerged in animal. All verb. All summons.
Resonant aether. It's the Black Slayer first. Plunging his fangs into
the shoulder's tensing muscle. Next Gasher. And last Tusk. Homeric
animal—lunging, murdering jaw. Cunning fucking dogs. Lashing out across
the mountain. First to maul: first to be praised. The stag their master
is down. Gyrus of his wild eyes. Law of death he registers. Its
gnostic instant. Fury of the pack quickly come. Slashing his hide. Piercing
every inch of flesh. Havoc of vulnus. Garish of wounds. Sound he makes:
no stag's, no man's. His buckled knees—a glimpse of prayer.
A master's supplication. The futile petitions of his crew.
Actaeon's absence: His mind's mad terminal dancing. And the dogs.
Thronging him on every side. Thrusting their muzzles in his flesh.
Mangling their master. Under the stag's false form. Only his wounds
quench the Moon-goddess's murderous luminous rage: rumor's
ambiguous violence. A summer rainstorm's incessant hiss and thunder.

After Ovid

TO REPLACE WAKING WITH REALIZATION

for Nathaniel Mackey

Rusty brown spores of the Goliath Webcap in calcareous Asian woodlands.

Slimy violet cap of the Bitter Bigfoot Webcap in old North American beechwoods.

Long black underground rhizomorphs, under the bark of fallen trees like bootlaces, of the Honey Fungus in a British garden.

Troops of Salt-Loving Mushrooms along a Scandinavian seashore.

Plastic-wrapped packages of Cultivated Mushrooms in all American supermarkets.

Litter-rotting habits of the Violet Domecap in chalk and limestone European woodlands.

Amatoxins of the Deadly Parasol in suburban backyards.

Unfortunate reputation for smelling bad of the Fetid Parachute on cast-off leaf litter.

Bioluminescent gills loaded with cytotoxins of the Jack O'Lantern *omphalotus illudens* in a mixed Michigan woods.

Ectomycorrhizal hyphae of the Copper Brittlegill in a montane conifer forest.

Hot, acrid flesh and gastroenteretic poisoning of the Sickener in Russian woodlands.

Flat, weakly depressed cap and characteristic spicy aroma of the American Mastutake in an Oregon pine woods.

Inedible redcap of the Flame Bolete in a Nova Scotia grove.

Uncertain true distribution of the King Bolete among broadleaf and conifers the globe over.

Six-sided pores on the bracket of the Hairy Hexagon on fallen roadside logs in Jamaica.

Bright yellow pigment and mildly hallucinogenic tea tonic of the Dyer's Mazegill in a Moravian mycologist's possession.

Smooth undersurface of the Leathery Goblet in an Indonesian tropical rainforest.

Thin, rubbery-gelatinous brackets of the Jew's Ear on the elder tree Judas Iscariot hanged himself from.

Intricately coalesced fronds of the nearly universal Earthfan on the ground at the base of trees the world over.

Coma and convulsions from the ibotenic acid and muscimol of the Panthercap in Siberian pasture land.

Cholesterol-lowering lovastatin in the laterally expansive tiers of the fruit bodies of the Oyster Mushroom on compacted straw bales in a cultivator's warehouse.

And last:

Little pointed Phrygian cap of the dung-loving Magic Mushroom clustered on a lawn of manured grass.

THIRTEENTH AMANITA ODE

Courser in the boreal forest belt. Receded icecap.
Permutated applications of singsong. Astral light of the midnight sun. Astral
light of the noonday darkness.
Before the art of distillation.
Before the means of storing berries
and the juices of berries. Before
the techniques of fermenting liquors.
Shamans and mushrooms. Spruces and birches.
Northern Eurasian reaches. Sunlight glancing
off the Bothnian Sea. *Koivu*. Birch. Rich voice. Curved core.
Listening
hard.

Ash. Spears of autumnal light. All yellow.
Like Pentecostal commas of flame.
Punctuating each head.
Acetylene *yod*. En-
theogenic fire.

And the human novum of forgiveness.

FOURTEENTH AMANITA ODE

I.

I saw anxiety the other morn,
it was a thick and coiled Satanic horn
    that in the night had torn
violent fissures in what the years had made
    of a life. How it played
habits of mind into a grisly noise
    all sense or call defies.
A decomposition. Falling apart.
    Things that once seemed an art.
Panics with no mysteries attending
    but whiffs of life's ending.
Rotten. Fronded. Slowly pulping the trees
    at their bases. With disease
parasitically supported. Life.
    Always there. Huge and fed off.

I I.

Rex of hymns forming songs: rheum of praise

a secret gland secretes, theoric,

heroic, human.

Semele slain by thunderbolt—

Athena's endless love for her—

Ino's deathless life beneath the sea—

Where is death for us? Nowhere clearly marked it seems.

No joy at the end of a quiet day

the Sun has carried for us—:

Streams of well being,

streams of dread.

Joys and

toils.

Always inward verging. Always coursed

by fate, indifferently surfing a curl of good fortune agitating

toward some sad reverse. Splashed with bliss.

Chronos sires the stars whose spent fires even he can't relight.

Luckless days and happy nights

fathom eventual forgetfulness

keen-eyed daughters of time daily embellish but love

insistently gushes over with oracles

of lasting feeling.

The Fury's vision. Wealth

rewarded for skills makes opportunities
ambition pushes the range of
into plutocratic acts. Truly the light of man
is this glowing star
of money. Stinking with sins
lawless and pious souls alike
—sinners in this realm of Zeus—
suffer rhadymanthine judgment
as harsh as hard to avoid
even if your money however stolen or earned
allows you to imagine the future:
the one below the Earth passes sentence
riddling your withering corpse with spores
you huff from piles he shoves at your mouth, and you so desperate for breath,
infecting you into a more rapid decay.
Nights like these, ours, forever.
Days of the glorious streaming sun.
Gifts of life. Great boons. The unintentional lawfulness of water.
Troubled Earth. Sea's foams. All.

Whatever your fortune your livelihood's empty.
Oaths. Sworn with good faith? Do you keep your word?
Gods honored grant days without weeping
to the piously averse. Who among us hasn't weakened in steadfastness?
Who hasn't one time bribed a god in prayer?

Days without weeping. Constant labor rather. Hard
to endure.

   But if you're decent
and you care for your soul, and you
recognize sin honestly; and if you survive three
lifetimes in either world—the astral or
the world of matter—then take God's way
to the Tower of Time where ocean winds
coil the Island of the Blessed
and the flowers of gold are fiery
and the trees on the shore are shining
and the waters are soaking them with life
and where with nimble fingers they bind the flowers and leaves into garlands
and where they sweep clean the place before the throne of Rhadymanthus,
and where God's holy bird, dawn's Ethiopian Sun,
sings daily morning's potent song
like an arrow newly sprung.

After Pindar

III.

A death cap's firm-fleshed fruit
clean white and pocked
with sunlight
picked
at risk

cap and stalk
thick
with lethal toxins.

But life springs from mycelium.
One day even your corpse will course with
flexuouse hyphae whose
saprophytic devourings will cleanse
your every mental cell of all the poisons
in waking life you harbored.

FIFTEENTH AMANITA ODE

MY WIFE'S COUGH

sounds like nothing else on Earth.

Seals trapped in an underwater cavern barking in unison.

Throbs of a chainsaw cutting into petrified cloud.

Sonograms of a witch's cauldron.

Pneumonia's dynamite. A puzzling, detonated speech form.

It's a violence in her esoteric core sounded out in nocturnal code, a phlegmy
   mesh of hexes whose tissue

mushrooms

might

abundantly

spring

from.

SIXTEENTH AMANITA ODE

KABIROI

To the fuller discussion of the Kabiric and Dactylic cults which I now believe to underlie
much of Orphic mysticism, I hope to return on some future occasion.

—Jane Ellen Harrison, *Prolegomena to the Study of Greek Religion*

Are you the earthly feet of the godhead?
Are you the gloomy forms emerging from the friction of soil and moisture?
Are you gods and demons churning the particulate milk of time?
Anxious ancient minds. Marvelous determinations.
Self-creation and uncertainty mounting in the transformations.

Vanished. Away. Toward Samothracian shores wreathed
with sycamores under whose shade they burrow, intensify.
What lust compels them to rush so singlemindedly to the high
kingdom of the Cabiri? They're little glomerous godlings.
The soul's delved spectacle: a pageant in their slow-motion meshing.
Ursystem's secret society they create never entirely knowing what they are.
Bright Moon! Stay. Thicken dusk with a silver starch of light. That day
might be warded and in the gloom we might thrive.
Dwarfish, shriveled, unspectacular bearer of these unruly compounds.
What should your appearance be to us? What new arts
do you bear up from the inaccessible treasure chamber?
What yolk of Moon from the egg of the gods?

SEVENTEENTH AMANITA ODE

MOLY

SYRIAN RUE   AFRICAN RUE

ESFAND   HARMEL

TURKISH RED   HAOMA

MOLY   MOLY   MOLY

MOLY   YLOM

peganum harmala

ruta graveolus

WILD RUE

for abortifacience
for alternativity
for ambecide
for anodyne
for aphrodesia
for diuresis

for emesis
for emmenagogery
for intoxication
for lactogogery
for narcosis
for soporesis
for stimulation
for sudoresis
for vermifuge

In moly there is an incantation, and in its steam there is a remedy for seventy-two diseases.

For shivering, write these things into a scroll and bind them to yourself.

For a molar that hurts, say: You are Axis, you are Abraxas, the angel who sits upon the Tree of Life

its surface redolent crimson

pocked with the tatters of its veil of birth.

For the treatment of a wound, together grind cumin, fennel, parsley, mastic, coriander, bayberries, almonds, pennyroyal, salt, and vinegar to mix with the mash from the fruit of a cypress. Boil it and then apply it.

For deception, lead your friends far from your secret stash, claiming the moly is just ahead.

For strain, take a coin of bronze, catch an iridescent fly. Write on a chit the first name in your prayer. Tap spores atop. Fill the eyes of the fly with drops of aged vinegar. Let it go. Coin under your tongue for a day.

For a quarrel, utter it over oil.

Anointings.

For a man, fill your right hand with crystals of salt to present before the Sun. Cast them over your head and sprinkle with honey water.

And for a second spell, for a week from when the Moon is full: molasses-juice of the "panacea weed," hartshorn, storax, mastic, calamus extract.

ABLANATHANALBA

ABRAXIEL

Uproot the magical spells AKRAMACHAMARI

AEEIOUO

AEEIOUO

AEEIOUO

ZODION

AOAOAO

Moly, spell-breaker. Beta-carbolines, harmine, and harmaline. A tonic. Extracted from the seeds.

Sedative. Narcotic. Mildly visual.

Good for the joints. Hazaian powers—drunkenness of a dancing ecstatic. Binder and encompasser.

Oneirophobia. Bearing the dream to the rhapsodic line.

Properties of drunkenness. Or mandala drawing.

Apotropaic ward of the evil eye.

Wild rue. Syrian dragon.

Mercurius. Feeling the intoxication of the demiurge.

Live embers. Obscure presentiment.

Like an imperfect metal plucked from the ground. Great

lobes of flesh. Black tangle of the roots.

Milky whiteness of the cap. Seen from a distance,

like a flower. Moly. Hard

for mortals to extract without breaking

but for a god like nothing.

EIGHTEENTH AMANITA ODE

Early spring's unruly over-
fecundation, that perfume-mash of June
weather, the blooming, taffy-scented star magnolia,
forsythias, crocuses, lilies the eye
requires time
to differentiate
but lacks—

the waxy sound of the ruffian wind. What stirs. In the earth.
Seriously. What fruits
in the soil's cereal drum prepare to push
up to the crust
to join into this sudden
hectic
life?

NINETEENTH AMANITA ODE

There are five hundred years to which the Tree of Life clings, generating verdure and offspring for the world. All the waters of Creation, drawn and flowing from the beginning, branch beneath it, through it.

—Zohar, *Be-reshit*

I.

Let the earth riot with a riot of living forms tithing
the tithe of the earth in tumults, its theotrophous abundances
secret springtime ceremonies augur. Tumular throngs. New souls
innovated on the throne of flame but yielded by
the orbiting lord of gloom. *It is a dual Earth, dualized*
by darkness and light. *Sinuosities of the meadows*, wilds of the woods.
Immense—*an immense and mighty tree*
entheogenic, supple in form. The left hand knows it. By touch.

Vivid earths. Vivid earths of the living. Antique instant: enveloping
everything in chaos. Unmentioned, hidden unknown at the dawntide.
    Threads,
weaving in the soil a recess, arousing in there an awe saprotrophs

knurl the lunging roots of in a high-hearted
oracle of the dead the great grooming tide of the spring
announces.

Nitid knot of smoke. Elastic ochre-yellow
force of ascid spores flashing forth like cooled
sparks. Emicant Lord of the Way, quivering
all of a sudden in streams of new light balanced
in a tuft of grass. Mysterious expansion of this point
of revealed darkness, breaking forth. Dozens of sudden mushrooms.
Crowding in the forest grasses. Gathering euphoria. All
the pitted caps. The collapsed tops of the spent fruits. Sporating invisibly.
Crawled spread mayapples carpet that morels verge
into, toward. Cryptogams. Each towering ash tree fruits
within the pressure of death.

II.
Tree of Life radiating life
Life that centaurs devour
Life in the open firmament of heaven
Life that autumn ceremonies occult
Life whose canopy is the adoring of the lower world by the upper world
Life that springs from a secret seedless source
Life that goes back very far
Life that awe and reverence summon by night

Life that dissolves the cells among omens
Life that never quits the things of this world
Life inventing air, space, ether, aura
Life that sifts siftings from the refuse
Life that is gathered up, viatical
Life the exact tonnage of whose fruit bodies taken from the forest is not
    entirely known
Life that grows from the stem
Lobed, toothed, compound life
Life of veins, life of throbs of water
Life robust in the springtide sunlight
Life engraved in the midnight soils
Life that bursts forth from the hidden supernal glooms
Life that shines, shining forth.

TWENTIETH AMANITA ODE

SECOND TATTERS

In a wind
the lake's scissoring surface

and the Sun's vernal glare
the gulls cut to curls
in their turns.

::

The lake's lurid blue
irises like crepe paper fringe.

::

Dragonflies in dozens of squadrons over grasses
stained in June sun
strobing

through teleportation
the headwinds are chasing.

TWENTY-FIRST AMANITA ODE

Night. Lord of all the Earth. Spreading from the left side of the light.
From whom the human image emerges. Noctivagitous
embracer of all images.

Light first radiated on the right side, darkness
on the left. Consummate radiance, high depth
of the issuing light. Angelophanic umber, shadow
of death, sponginess that the light slows into—
the expanding scribal matrix
expands

like an awesome ice,
like a horrible crystal
nighttime colors.

Listen: lurid ear of the earth.
Watch: Earth burying earth.
Watch: Earth piling earth

under an undular crease
the cream of a storm pours down

blots of rain bruise.

Here is a mystery in detail. When darkness aroused, it aroused intensely.
Arrayed in an array, sacronymic amanites
micronic powder-white spores shake down from.

Human beings are new every day.
The world below their striding limbs seethes
with fiery-liquid darkness.
With sealed concealments of threaded extensiveness.
Who revives the dead? Night, collector of the darkness waters.
Who controls the Moon? Night, through whom darkling fruits all the
    networks
unite.

After the radiance of the night's great light has faded,
after the density of primordial night has been treasured away,
a form coheres from the earthen fabric,
a catacosmic egg
all concealed within.

Night detonates an emanationism
theurgic Earth encloses
up through shadow
rung to rung

throng
to
throng.

This speech
deriving from the side of darkness
reveals depths.

And every soul of the living beings, who glides—
who swarms—
six wings—

Who is she? Night.
And what were you doing? I was gazing
upon the secrets of creation.

I.

Unlumined mass emanating into the hidden catacosm
caligated dampness seeps everywhere into
undoing drought. Good snows. Everywhere, points
of radiance concealed. Birdsong
in pre-dawn. Bird and weird—a magical firebird with brilliant plumage
a dream ensnares in a hollow
pit. Moon in slow-motion flash, fading.

In the lifemass, an iliaster
masking sinewed extensions plying
earth. In the mind, a chlorophyll
conferring the faculty of feeding on light, even
its cryptogametic looseners.

In the dawn, a wintry sign: a pulvurulent brown
sigh of humus waking up.

II.

Three channels root the dead tooth to the socket a waning nerve throbs in
whose death your jaw aches in sympathy with great
gushes of pain emanate onto one live tooth after another.

III.

Immensely pervasive stain of demonism!
Firm and fragrant flaws.

Serpent who injected slime into Eve who absorbed it.
From the left side of darkness all the haunts of maleficent species:
demons, goblins, sorcerers, spirits. Humans, too.
Demons of consummation.
Demons of diphtheria.
The body, absorbed in a whirlpool.
The humors of the body, absorbed by a dry powder.

Woe to humans, who do not see!
Obtuse. Unaware how full the world is of
strange, invisible creatures. Of hidden things.
If humans could see things as they are, they
would be amazed that they endure.
See what?

Hexes in incessant meshes.
Daylight in dangerous radium.
Disdain from the deep-zoned muses.
Our ignorant, tragically flawed deaths everywhere creeping
the Earth we keep as our shithouse.

HIDDEN STONE

Vision of the unspeakable cosmos of signs hidden
in the hyphal somaphoria. *What*
stirred? What did I see?
I saw the mesocosm in the Earth itself,
the stones whose living tissues it bodies forth
alive in ways unlike any other form of life.

I saw shadow intensify as gloom
new to the thatched and crosshatched surface of
things—network of tree roots, thrum of Sun the
euphoria of the foray enriches into panoramas of sense
ready to assent that the heart of the faithful
is the throne of revelation hewn from secret stone. Light does not get
old; neither does gloom. Horrid vacuity bottomless.
Recluse, unsummoned power
avid energies attend to await. So

turn to the woods, the Oregon shore line, and
enter the pines
rising along the upthrust sandy hillocks and

rush to loose
a rock-hard lordling, the first
edular phoenix-form,

reticulated stem fat as a grapefruit
early yet in its short life,
cap tucked in, penile, burnished a soft brown—
total godling.
I saw this one. And then another. And one after the next
for the next seven hours.
I saw them revealed close by and then far away,
colossal and pygmy. This is the song of the hidden stone possessing
a thousand forms.
None newer none more ancient than this one.
Dragon form—
Ouroboral form the juices of Asclepius anoint—.

I saw King Boletes in Templar droves
none more legendary than those this day discovered.
Visions: dazzling, brilliant, lustrous, psycholithic, flaming.
Elementary shadow: creaturely kingdom.
Note the energy entering the song with the
image of the mushroom sculpted with Cycladic control
entering the archaic tissue of the living nature
Soma's strange reef-like structure ensures.

Oregon.
Caul of cloudhang. October
cumulus,
undular wavestream the Pacific modulates,
lapis of hidden dusk the undershadow
tilths in earth.
Umbered morsel. Kinesis of an energetic system
momentum coils and uncoils.

Lapidary premonitions: sky, water—earthen thearchies
activate the angel. Pores.
Pores, and not gills, do the breathing.
I saw as an abstract understanding millions of micron-sized pores
droning in shook cascades, dusting down
essence, pulver of earth lighter than air, creator of vital force,
mycelium—manifestor—monarch.

::

Vision: no more than this?
But this is the total encounter, to which
the soul aspires.

Incipit: for those who have the living symbol. The passage is easy.

Soma: from whose inmost core
stonify then burst forth the purest lodes
of euphoria, and in the Moon's lurid signal
its mossy masses erupt
with fruiting lifeforms while among the mesmerizing
shadows the daytime forest—ferning
with mysterious light—orients its
shining knobs.

Intoxication: and the emeto-cathartic effect of Soma.

There: is the hidden stone. Antler and tongue. The stone in occultation. It is a
    materia
prima. It is an original fire. An elemental cordial. It is permanent
water, said to be the original material of the stone. The water
has a thousand names. The stone has a name too dense to sound.
It condenses into a core in the Earth's center. In which
is Eternity. Regenerating. An intricate affilial network of Eternity. It expands
in soils into the tilth of the earth. And there it meets Eternity
again. Both within the earth and without. And the abstract fact of it
is the yellowing mystery, its tincture. And the actual
pursuit of its euphoric somalosis—the elation of the foray.
There are the woods. And the Oregonian ocean, heaving. *The land
of woven labyrinths*. The woods absorbing echoes. *The land of clouds*.

A sheet of gunship cloudhang, flares of morning light at the edges.
The land of the region of waters. The channels of the earthen tendrils.
The solids underneath the pine tufa. *A concave Earth*
wondrous, Chasmal, Abyssal, Incoherent but suddenly lucid.
Suddenly legible—one boletus anticipating the next—a projection
of some future's core. There are the woods. And there are we. Early morning.
Sunlight temblors are fall's upsurging insistences. First,
one bolete. An old mushroom. But perfect. And then another one—
this one young. Truly perfect. Mahogany sheen of the cap. Reticulated
cream of the stem. *The Sun giants into the Earth.* And dozens more
appear. Citrinitine stones. Lords of a holy yellow. Somalithic nodes
the woods' umber inundates with gloomy energies. There are the woods.
And the man with the dogs. And the discovery of the twins—a
mushroom anvil smote by dusk's lure into light while the man
with the dogs rambles on. About freedoms. Work. (Meth?) Incoherent.
    Chasmal. And the shadows yield
more. And keep yielding more. Earth is best. Loam alluminor.
An esotericism of the actual. Antler and tongue. Soma's acrodromous doxeme.

Autrey: explored the edge of euphoria, filling it with living form
excited half-sleep deprived him of. We ate breakfast in an October
false dawn, waiting for usable daylight.
The parking lot—discrete placement of the car
so as not to attract attention. What were we doing there?

No one should know.

                      And with light, into the dune grass
and the pine woods thickening just beyond. First
one bolete—a perfect bun—and then quickly another.
And within minutes the dynamosis of instasy—: dozens
more. All reveal. One cousin fungus gesturing
toward the next. Hours pass in euphoric
foray. One great lord showing forth after
another. The twins conjoined. The god's sledge. The effigy.
The living form. By day's end, seventy pounds.
Diffused light daylong. Suspiring ocean
hissing alongside. *The real mystery does not
behave mysteriously or secretively; it speaks a secret language.*

::

*Thou
hast conceived the greater
for we have opened the gates unto thee.*

The Sun
drowning in the fountain of Mercury. The illusion
possessed of informing
power. The birth

of the stone, its graphite debris.
Which the whole world has before its eyes
yet knows not.

The salt
of wisdom at the physical center
of the Earth. The artifex, fishing for Neptune. Dowsing
for the hidden stone. Secret contents
of the Work. *It is assumed that a species of*
magical power capable of transforming even brute matter
dwells in the human mind. And in the forests of Oregon.
And Michigan. And Lower Austria.

Spagyric opus

yet of
simple
ether

whose fiery pneuma
reaches up to the Seat of the Lord.

An incorrupt medicament,

the stone is a spiritual stone.
The stone is a volatile stone.
The stone is a sublime stone.

The subtle body comes to life.
The supercelestial body comes to life

in a dusk,
a darkness,
a loam.

The soul is the vice-gerent of God.
The soul is a mycelial antler.
A secret tongue.

By this you have seen the secrets
of the Earth hidden in plain sight. You can understand
what the Book of Concealment has said about the Creation; what
manner of body the fruit of the Earth had before and after the Fall,
what the agitated energy was, what the knowledge
foretold, what the birch is and what the pines are, and
what matter of fruit was eaten in Eden, and in what emerging bodies
life is newly resurrected, and how the little puffs of spore powder
travel, and in what living form we receive this knowledge,
and how to cook it
and how it tastes.

CODA

What did I see? Afterwards, lying that night in my bed,
the involuntary retinal inventions flickering scene after scene
repeated agarical discoveries, what's hidden within
brought forth from the Earth's sentient core, there,
imaginal, scene after scene,
and a settling wellness that plumes
upward into sleep
the night of the Earth interpenetrates
and overarches.

TWENTY-THIRD AMANITA ODE

The great spastic glass of the Sun
in winter's going glare.

::

Wind's antic helicoid
winding upward through the tree.

Agitations.

A
web's
sinews'
yellow
radiance.

::

Circles of wind rapture
the young hawk flashes through.
A robin's nest she stops
to plunder.

::

Easter Moon
that blooms above a reef of cream.

Vernal silver the house is steeped in.

::

Soaring vulture's shadow dowsing
the hillside's sunlight—

in which others are roosting. Wings in hieroglyph
a glossy pitch
engraves.

::

I need that noonday Moon
hanging in the sky.

::

The sawing strokes a warbler sings.

::

What is this
anteworldly lunar syrup
spores of life course along
cresting through the thawed crust
mayapples like seaside parasols shelter
in spring shade?

::

An oriole narrating his involvement with some blossoms.

::

That house sparrow splash landing in the lilacs.

::

August evening's earlier ending
when thought itself sublimes.

::

Talk's vanishing esses in the cicadas' cycling ratchets.

::

New Day Rising

Sun on pine.
Morning's glittering indices.

"This stuff is Ice Age."

::

Those
bluejays'
new day's
relayed
jeers.

::

Waning lustrous late autumnal Sun—
wind's distant engine roar.

::

Three monostiches

    I. Lakeshore's bluish dusk mid-November dims down.

    II. That's the lake's glaucous glass a cormorant's invisible vortex scratches.

    III. An accidental eternity the lake's waves swell with mist enlumes in aerosol.

OCHRE VAULT

[Ceremonial Fiftieth Amanita Ode]

for John Tipton

I. RIDDLES

First

I saw four fine creatures linked in weird communion
a fir tree fixed in an affinity of shadow
earth emanates. They were an emanation of earth,
earth arising from an earthen throne
smoothed into a bun-shaped stone.

Second

Forth from the earth, honeycomb caps cluster
where grasses in spots of sunlight newly tuft:
wonderful creatures watching the mulch
supple-minded lookers miss
alarmed by the sound of a snipe's skyward bliss.

Third

I fed in the deep working foam of the earth:
loam covered me I inched through.
Cooled and slowly warmed I probed soils tenderly.
Footless, I'm crowned. My flesh is meat for a man.
My appearance is a slow-motion gush, with force to lift
a cobblestone. My finder will fix me with salt
and garlic. Best to eat me hastily but cooked. Say what I am called.

II. L

When the letter L which signifies the Deeps by itself is engrained in every
    spore of the earth.
When L is the alveolar lateral approximant in the alphabet of things.
When L is in the language by which you apprehend and through which you
    enthuse a divine omniscience.
When L laces every porous tubule gametes strobe from like sugar shook
    from a caster.
When L is in the name of the Sun.
When L begins the name of the Moon.
When L is one of seven symbols that cover all possible numeric variations.
When L seethes in the beasts of the sea writhing toward Earth to be born.
When L is the leveler of air, the shoveler, the howler all three.
When L is lava's solid fire.
When L is the lode of the earth.

When L is the liquid that burns into speech forms dynamic in vitality but
    unbalanced in endurance.
When L unlearns lore in favor of knowledge.
When L unbinds love radicalizing its reaches.
When L is within the Ochre Vault.

III. THE DEPTH

Though the clustering of wrinkled peaches is the sign of the arborist's talents.
Though the mushrooms are talented devourers.
Though the Lord made an agaricus in the ancient pine forests and his
    disciples made a ritual meal.
Though the angels of God took it out of his hand and buried it in the Depth.
Though no one can have an outward life who does not give generously to the
    inward life.
Though there is no Depth in which there are not hyphae or funguses.
Though the mushrooms inspire the senses, chiefly in their musking scent.
Though the fruit perplexes the vegetable order and the roots tenaciously
    decompose all adversaries.
Though the boletes have their angels even the Latin of God's taxonomy.
Though the warp and the woof of agarics are worked by perpetual degrading
    energies.
Though morels are good for both the living and the dead.
Though there is a language of mushrooms.
Though there is a euphoria of foraging upon many mushrooms.
Though obsolete phrases are arguably a poetry of the resurrection.

Though mushrooms are an antique medicine.

Though mushrooms are musical in olfactory harmonies.

Though the right names of the mushrooms abide in the earth. God make
mycologers better vocabularians.

after the Exeter Book and Christopher Smart

TWENTY-FIFTH AMANITA ODE

If you ask, "How did the earth?" The answer is: Human beings constitute the essence of earth—they ruin the earth and she is ruined.

—Zohar, *Noah*

Woe the destroyer's eye absorbs, destroyer of the world. In the days of our
    becoming. Wilderness surrounded us. Now
we surround the wilderness.

Obliterated.
Deleted.
Blotted out.
Destroyed.

Annals of political decay.
The scripture of starvation.
The wicked abounding in the world. Our
spiritual destitution. Plutocrats in jet packs. What else is there?
Birds of Heaven. Beasts of the fields. Surging in waves of migration. Why

annihilate in one happy stroke all of these
along with the wicked, who deserve it? What kind of Mahdi
occulted in a telescopic *futurum* would gaze backward
into our moment
and not recognize the workings of redemption?

Sweet old world. Stripped bare.
Stained in evil.
The choice of evil. Imagining evil.
The residue of evil clinging to everything.

God. Colossally remote in holiness.
Who will return the world to earth, as it originally was.
Earth intermingled with earth, as has been said.
From now on, he will thrash the angels in the air
with unrelenting light. The world

is both good and evil and yet neither, the matrix
of all possibilities. The *Gloria mundi* quarried
in primordial foretime was a bitter salt, mostly
black and evil smelling. The spirit
of chaos cannot be distinguished from the Holy Spirit.
Visionary gleam.
Clarity.

Clarity in the absolute garden.
The sweet horror of myrrh.
A lunar-terrestrial substance, stained with salt.
Can the incorruptible nature of the spirit survive?

When the wicked abound in the world, waters
vanish from the sea and rivers run brackish with
the bitter salts of chaos. And the land
is drenched by supernatural
saturation.

The God of compassion
and the God of destruction
are one.

Woe to human beings who do not know
or see. They are all contumelious fools, unaware
of how full the world is of strange, invisible
creatures whose lives arise from hidden things.
If their eyes were opened, they would be beaten breathless at
how they themselves endure.

TWENTY-SIXTH AMANITA ODE

FIRST OF APRIL/LAST TATTER

That wind coming from the Sun. A controlled burn
reaches the still-thawing prairie.
A ruby-crowned kinglet.
Passing through.

TWENTY-SEVENTH AMANITA ODE

ENVOI

Clarity.
Clarity in the absolute garden.
A sweet horror of myrrh.
A damp mirror of earth.

SECRET INSCRIPTION

Greetings, elemental lords, hyphic hairs dewy along the oriental ochre gates, greetings, entire substructure of daemonic earth, greetings, daemon that penetratest from the catacosm to the mesocosm, from Midgard to Eden, and from Earth, which abideth in the midst of the universe and its soil, to uttermost bounds of the abyss, which it salteth and signeth with softness, greetings, daemon that ensoils in me mineral epoxies ... Greetings, beginning and end of decomposing Nature, greetings, thou who burrowest through the element that untiringly covers the cauldron at the core, greetings, magnetic sun inside the earth, whose sauna mythologizeth to the world, greetings, Moon shining in the fable with fickle silvery radiance, greetings all ye attendant daemons advancing in harmonious subservience ... O great, greatest inapprehensible meshing of the world, formed into a clod of ripe earth! ... dwelling in aetherial tilth, having the form of flesh in magnificent lobes, of earth, of elements, but of earth most of all, of darkness, of umber, of phosphorescent night glimmer, damp-fiery-humid daemon!

INVOCATION

Terra speculum est.
Agaricus caelum mirrorest.

TWENTY-EIGHTH AMANITA ODE

TATTERS/ADDENDA AND POSTSCRIPTS

ADDENDA

That yellow's belted decibels ebullient sunlight broadcasts into the open air.

::

The *kekking* of the Caspian terns drawn
along in a strong north wind
portends
crisis; or,
the Earth revolving.
Great throbs of the lake
churned slate into a milk
of late summer. In a dream
you receive a stack of packages and letters
from everyone important to you.

The Sun is a great brass undulum.
A chicken mushroom fruiting from a fallen log
flames ludicrous orange.

What tenets does this work endure?
What looking weaves with the wind-drawn waters
the pattern you can live by
as the intensities of age set in?

::

Midewin

The wind's river the grasses hiss at.
Dickcissal.
Monarchs.
Wild bergamot's crushed blue Kleenex.
Blue
jays'
loose
jeers.
Lurid velvet of the red-headed woodpecker's
strobing
flash.

::

Septembrine sheet of light cloudhang gauzes.

::

POSTSCRIPTS

Clods of turf in a pile from far off
like the pelt of a bear.
And still
near.

::

A rough-gusting vernum of waves
mergansers core scant warmth from, mating
kept for a moment
in check.

::

Shelf ice's soft rustle—

a still grammar wintering gulls
punctuate in terse shifts

along
the dynamic
fringe.

Caves
of ice
we trace.

A boy's
burred
thrill.

TWENTY-NINTH AMANITA ODE

TOADSTOOL

The belief that [mushrooms] are formed from the harmful substances of the earth and the venom of toads and that fungi always grow in places where toads abound, and give shelter to them when they take the air. —John Ramsbottom, *Mushrooms & Toadstools*

I suggest that the "toadstool" was originally the fly-agaric in the Celtic world; that the "toadstool" in its shamanic role had aroused such awe and fear and adoration that it came under a powerful tabu, perhaps like the Vogel tabu where the shamans and their apprentices alone could eat of it and others did so only under pain of death; that people hesitated to pronounce the very name of this mushroom, so that in time it became nameless and the name it formerly carried hovered thereafter ambiguously over the whole fungal tribe so that all the mushroom world fell under the same floating tabu. This tabu was a pagan injection belonging to the Celtic world. The shamanic use of the fly agaric disappeared in time, perhaps long before the Christian dispensation. But in any case the fly-agaric could expect no quarter from the missionaries, for whom toad and toadstool alike were the Enemy. —R. Gordon Wasson, *Soma: The Divine Mushroom of Immortality*

I.
the throne of the toad
the pileus of the mushroom, its leaf
"the foule toade"
Mycenean liquor

slime and excrescence
the knobbed body
the fungal structure
the magical texture
the crimson-and-fleece cluster
the infra-red luster
the club-footed one
the splay-footed one
the limping one
the lethal aura
the fool's mushroom

II.
What if the god is a mushroom after all?

And resurrection is a spoor.

The Tree of Life is bracketed with punk.
From touchwood all the holy khans are descended.
Fuming pulp is seer.

A birch tree.
It holds the punk to light the fire the body hides whose sparks unsoul it.
"Why don't all the flies die?"
"No worries. They are sure to die later."

The roots of the birch tap into the lake of the Waters of Life
overflowing with the tawny-yellow milk from the breasts of the fly agaric.

The roots of the towering Siberian birch.
Flies consuming the stinkhorn's mucus.
What are the forms of life?
What are the dominant forms of mystery unfolding for you to understand?
What will be the last little thing purring through your awareness?
What will be its magnitude in comparison to your keenest moments?

Behold the toadstool.
Earth-magical force thriving in wicked lore.
Saffron plenty in a Michigan pine woods.
The umbrella of Nicholas.
Delicate strokes of a French illustration, sylvan softness of a dangerous
    agarical scene.
Mycochthonomous toadstool.
Dynamochthonomous toadstool.
Disobedient toadstool.
Of shining and wrinkled knowledge.

III.
Malodorous moths sooth dolorous oaths
mortals almost shout out. Doom
shrouds

moults
dorsal atoms
loom aloud.

Great root
emitting light.

It is thru the todestool that he kenneth the deep's abysses

THIRTIETH AMANITA ODE

PINDARIAN EPIMETHEUS

I. ELYSIUM

The Sun throbbing life.

The world below—oiled in night.

Meadows galax and spiderwort lavender; incense trees shading the pathways

leading to the city, golden

cloud fruit

they hang with.

Some of them taking pleasures with horses

and some of them resting in lusty allure.

Some of them drinking great draughts of new wine

and some of them tapping the strings of their lutes.

Thus blooms bliss

like this.

Incense fumes around the cores

of the far-shining fires

alongside the altars of agonized gods.

And from the other side
a flume of darksome night unabating.

II. VISIONARIES

Grace to see the end of the world beneath a hollow of earth—
God can cause an unpolluted light to come to life
in blackest night.
And gloom to shroud unsullied noon.
When mortal life ends, a god's begins.

Nothing cursed, nothing altered.
Not of the earth that bears gifts
nor the sea that rushes wildly out.

THIRTY-FIRST AMANITA ODE

TELEIDOSCOPE

THE PROBLEM: RUPTURE

And now I, forethought's decaying fullness, rich in earth and tilth, shaped myself into my offspring. We exist alongside every woodland path.

> We are the elemental dewfall, earth's first fruiting lobes.
> We are the spores of a fullness
> a memory of ungraining.

I travel in an underearth realm of great darkness verging forward until I enter the chambers where darkness awakens. The temptations of chaos in me unflex from long-threaded manacles, and I devour death, a lover.

I returned, I, the anticipation of an ecophanic onset, sporated on a wind that agitates all matter.

From within, I draw up a darkness, wild-scented and textured like pine needles. The underworld opened up, shrugging off its cloak.

The foundations of chaos—tremoring within. Breathing powers— whispering in the motions. Hidden things. In motion and in stillness.

The root of the light is a coil of darkness. Reaching earliest earth.
We are the dark forms dwelling in darkness.
We fruit a fullness
deliquescing the darkness.

I entered the darkness and threaded the underearth with silky mold.
The prison of life is movelessness. As death's devourer, I am motion and I
am rest. The imprisoner of living forms stands still, becoming spiritually
entombed.
Again, I went forth, extending the work of darkness.

We are the darkness expanding in darkness.
We are the spores of a fullness,
a memory of decay.

I brightened my face with bioluminescent threads of night, tilth's realm
compressed and released from an earthen home.
I said, the masters are speaking of a deep sleep. The masters abundantly
everywhere. There is a cramp in the darkness. A small wild spasm. It con-
tracts like a birth-pang that grows more wrenching through the night.

THE SOLUTION: SALVATION
Since it feeds on the theophanic forms,
an earthen soul of life it deepens, even as it throbs
like an allegory.

Transmigratory matter in these tendrils signals
an epochal act of eschaton
God vindicates in creation. We are the darkness
expanding in lurid
gloom the mushroom's
teleidoscope views
as a complete ecology of the resurrection—

purposeful decay,
shining darkness,
nourishing soil.

THIRTY-SECOND AMANITA ODE

UULDURFADUR

I.

Our life. Anew. The thought of fear. In the forest of darkness.

Finding myself. Lost there.

Its wildness.

Its roughness.

Its harshness.

In the dark of that woods. All gloom taking shape.

What will you form from it,

taking it in your hands?

Loam-grown uuldurfadur.

Wonderworking wuldorfaeder.

Glorious fashioner of beginnings.

Shining night.

Overhead.

In the Moon's lustered omen

quilts
of tissue
clustered
in mixed woods
unlume
and red oaks

solemnize symbiosis

archaic querents shift over

for traces of that original mace,
an ancient unconsuming taste.

Your one-time word
is a spirit lord

become the summonings
of the end of things.

II. FUNDAMENTUM PRIMUM

jasper
sapphire
chalcedony (agate)
beryl

topaz
chrysoprase
jacinth
amethyst

an angel's breadth
a lamb's lamp
a moon fruit's superb jewels.

THIRTY-THIRD AMANITA ODE

I. INSTRESS/OUTLEASE

Instress is the most mysterious and potent of all of Gerard Manley Hopkins's inventive coinages, aligned closely with another, *inscape*. Instress means something like a manifestation of a thing's being. The word appears in a notebook Hopkins kept in 1866 as an undergraduate at Balliol College, amid a set of meditations on the Pre-Socratic philosopher Parmenides, the essence of whose philosophy runs: "For to think and to be are one and the same" (in Stanley Lombardo's translation). This collision of being and thinking inspired Plotinus to write, "'Knowing and Being are one thing,' [Parmenides] says, and this unity is to him motionless in spite of the intellection he attributes to it: he compares it to a huge sphere in that it holds and envelops all existence and that its intellection is not an ongoing act but internal" (in Stephan MacKenna's translation). Hopkins intuits much of this himself when, in February 1868, he writes, "All words mean either things or relations of things."

In "Parmenides," Hopkins is more expressive. He writes, "[Parmenides's] great text, which he repeats with more religious conviction, is that Being is and Not-being is not—which perhaps one can say, a little over-defining of his meaning, means that all things are upheld by instress and are meaningless without it." Hopkins was writing these notes during the time he decided to terminate his confessions within the Anglican Church and to convert to Catholicism, something—despite the convictions that compelled him to do it—that would cause the members of his family great pain.

Upheld by instress. The prepositional suffixes in those words hold all the relational meaning: *up, in.* In a felicitous observation, scholar Bernard McGinn, wanting to clarify the meaning of the word *anagogy* in the context of Christian mysticism, suggests that it means "uplifting," writing, "uplifting is really more like 'instressing,'" such that the soul's spiritual energy is buoyed by its activation in God's creative outpouring. So, instress is uplift, a thing's inherent buoyancy recognized in a perceiver's soul.

Among the ten preparatory stanzas in "The Wreck of the Deutschland," written in 1875, the ones in which Hopkins spells out his theology, which is more like a gash of light than a set of claims, he envisions Christ as instress, spied on the underside of the horizon, emblazoned with starlight:

> I kiss my hand
> To the stars, lovely-asunder
> Starlight, wafting him out of it; and
> Glow, glory in thunder;
> Kiss my hand to the dappled-with-damson west:
> Since, tho' he is under the world's splendor and wonder,
> His mystery must be instressed, stressed;
> For I greet him the days I meet him, and bless when I understand.

Glory in thunder, yes, but also something—a mystery—seen in the maculate western horizon, to be uplifted.

What Hopkins sees instress in most readily are clouds. One of Hopkins's greatest poems, "That Nature Is a Heraclitean Fire and of the Comfort of the Resurrection," begins with a high-hearted praise of clouds unmatched in English-language poetry:

> Cloud-puffball, torn tufts, tossed pillows | flaunt forth then chevy on
> an air-
> built thoroughfare: heaven-roysterers, in gay-gangs | they throng: they
> glitter in marches.

Hopkins prepared for this outburst of insight in his journals, which are replete with rapturous, incisive, comprehensive descriptions of the clouds he saw, seeing in them absolute instress:

> April 22 (1871)—But such a lovely damasking in the sky as today I never felt before. The blue was charged with simple instress, the higher, zenith sky earnest and frowning, lower more light and sweet. High up again, breathing through wooly coats of cloud or on the quoins and branches of the flying pieces it was the true exchange of crimson, nearer the earth / against the sun / it was turquoise, and in the opposite south-western bay below the sun it was clear oil but just as full of color, shaken over with slanted flashing 'travelers' all in flight, stepping one behind the other,

their edges tossed with bright raveling, as if white napkins were thrown up in the sun but not quite at the same moment so that they were all in a scale down the air falling one after another to the ground.

Instress as something you've never felt before.

At the same time, Hopkins was inventing an instressed language for the description of clouds, adapting Latin and Anglo-Saxon words for the purposes of vivid clarity: grains, loaves, burl, frown, wool, groom, turf, sod, fur. The clouds manifest as revealed forms of knowing and being in the novel unison of an old language:

April 21 (1871)—We have had other such afternoons, one today—the sky a beautiful grained blue, silky lingering clouds in flat-bottomed loaves, others a little browner in ropes or in burly-shouldered ridges swanny and lustrous, more in the zenith stray packs of a sort of violet paleness. White-rose cloud formed fast, not in the same density—some cooked and swimming in a wan whiteness, the rest soaked with the blue and like the leaf of a flower held against the light and diapered out by the worm or veining of deeper blue between rosette and rosette.

These descriptions are mesmerizing, and Hopkins was committed to them utterly. His journal entries from this time, during which he was in his late twenties and not so long after his conversion, record brightness, wind, shadow, shapes of cloud, chalkstrokes of light.

They are also anomalous, idiosyncratic. In 1802, Luke Howard, physician and amateur meteorologist, presented a paper to a small scientific club in London, the Askesian Society, entitled, "On the Modification of Clouds," which presented his classification system for clouds, making use of an ingenious set of Latin names for what he was seeing in the sky. This system involves two primary categories of cloud: heaps and layers. Each of these is observed in one of three tiers or levels, from low to middle to high. *Cumulus* means heap; *stratus* means flattened out. *Cirrus* is a tuft of horsehair. *Nimbus* refers to a precipitating cloud. (It's an adaptation of the Latin word for the cloud of downpouring splendor surrounding a god.) And *altus* refers to height. These five terms, individually or in combination, describe every main kind of cloud in Howard's classification system. Cirrostratus clouds are the wispy trails of ice crystals layering the highest portion of the sky. Cumulonimbus clouds are the great cadmium and shadow masses towering upward crowding the top of the sky and often bearing rain.

It's an excellent, flexibly adaptable system of meteorological observation the world over continues to rely on daily. But not once does Hopkins utilize any of Howard's language. It's possible that Howard's terminology was kept in the mouths of specialists. Nevertheless, it feels strange not to find any of these words in Hopkins. Here's his take on cumulonimbus clouds: "Later / moulding, which brought rain:. . . the frets, which are scarves of rotten cloud bellying upwards and drooping at their ends and shaded darkest at the brow or tropic where they double to the eye, and the whiter field of sky shewing between" (April 18). And here is Hopkins describing fair-weather altocumulus: "Very clear afternoon; a long chain of waxen delicately moulded clouds just tinged with yellow / in march behind Pendle. At sunset it seemed to gather most of it in one great bale." It's a curious omission in Hopkins's journal. His imagination seems optimally suited for Howard's nomenclature. Why this absence. I can only speculate, but I suspect that instress and its uplift are experienced in a unison so complete, only a language of experience suffices, and not an adopted language of observation.

The atmosphere belongs to an energetic system fed by the Sun but for practical purposes enclosed. This means that whenever violent weather occurs, clear and calm weather prevails somewhere else as part of a consequential relationship. Think of the sky after a storm passes through. In *The Old Man and the Sea*, Hemingway writes, "...when there are no hurricanes, the weather of the hurricane months is the best of all..." Hopkins's observations of clouds and the language he summons to appreciate them amount to a reverence, in the purest sense, for the energetic system to which the clouds belong:

> At eight o'clock about sunset hanging due opposite the house in the east the greatest stack of cloud, to call it one cloud, I ever can recall seeing. Singled by the eye and taken up by itself, it was shining white but taken with the sky, which was strong hard blue, it was anointed with warm brassy glow: only near the earth it was stunned with purplish shadow. The instress of its size came from comparison not with what was visible but with the remembrance of other clouds . . .

Instress is memory and form, the motion of the gaze from ground to sky to sacred canopy and to ground again. "It is the terror and beauty of phenomena, the 'promise' of the dawn and the rainbow, the 'voice' of the thunder, the 'gentleness' of the summer rain, the 'sublimity' of the stars, and not the physical laws which these things follow, by which the religious mind continues to be most impressed. . ." (William James, *The Varieties of Religious Experience*). Instress is meteoric, like a cardinal's flash of red. *Meteoros*, Greek for "raised," "lofty"; Aristotle coined meteorology to be the study of celestial phenomena—things aloft in the sky. Uplifted. Instressed. Celestial manifestation of creation's bright terrible power.

At root, this manifestation must include the earth. Heaven's cerulean blue is mirrored in earth's richest umber. The earth absorbs all that atmospheric energy, releasing it in growth and decay.

As clouds of air are transient showings of *instress* and *uplift*, clods of earth are slow-moving bodyings forth of *outlease* and *downspread*, antonymic twins.

As clouds are to the sky, so clods—especially in the form of mushrooms —are to the earth.

Instress and outlease, uplift and downspread describe the total planetary energetic system, integrating and unintegrating their appearances. And language is the field of manifestation.

II. CLOUD/CLOD

The god of cloud rolls into the blue.
Vast padding of the Sun
burns a dull fuse above. Low
overhang a jet creases
with engine roar, its
torn
sound.

> Cunningly foraged fungal load
> the larvae of the wood-boring ambrosia beetle
> feeds on rather
> than the cellulose and lignin themselves.

Brilliant cadmium towers of bleached flour.
Luteous ungluing of the light.
Later, rain clouds in layered qualms.

> Sabbath
> a witches' butter's jelly fruiting
> on a worn door frame
> hexes.

High pressure morning blue
translucency tissues on
ghost-thrown, glacial rags of air.

Sky in tatters
the wind scatters
weird
cream of light
enlumes.

A nimbus.
A cloud.
Some sod.
A sward.
Some turf.
A health of earth
epochal riots of the fungal nimbus
activate—

avalanching peat of cumular white
loaves and buns of mahogany stones.

Sky's high fur of ice
shagged ruins and bellowing meshes
puff upward into.
Everywhere the air's
lacy forms
without
duration.

The earth's clodded textures the soul mines.
Stipe,
volva,
gill,
spore,
wart,
wood.
Natural light.

Thin mass of stretched tripe with
thistle-blue undersides.

Squeezes of wisped vapor.

Field of gauze the light streams through,
the Sun a brass whisper.

Panther's spotted manna
gathered up in the sacred dawn.

High lumbering gunmetal massings
chicory tattering highlights.

Loosestrife's fuchsia candlewicks
uplifting milkweed's rainstoop.

Weft and mesh of cloudhang.

Weave and lease of garden soils—
sand, sun, bunch of earth
knuckled
into growth.
A persistent membrane's
chlorine
waft.

Gloam and form an earthworm foregrounds
A far-flown fire dragon's excellence
Forest wood's burrowing law
Surging blue cream daytime's raiment garments
In the earth house, an ancient legacy
Immense and precious
Loft and wonder

Wily soil's
woven secret's
uneven allure—
Cunning's umber, cobalt's heaped transfigured white.

III. SAY CLOUDS/SAY EARTH

Say clouds like seers draw closed the silver drape and
say clairvoyant blue is pierced
by Homeric spears of light tipped in epic bronze.
And say birds of prey like rags of smoke make
noonday zodiacs shudder
plumes of wind
bruise with ceaseless outlease
clouds like druids forecast in nature's torn oracles.
Clouds like a weeping child.
Clouds like a damask froth.
What you think towers into a beam of sunlight topples
into pashed foam, golden forms.
A sign of life life radiographs with avid sun cruised down in a blue
oblivion reflects in giddy volley.

::

Your dream of clouds is a vision of the poem.
Your feel of the earth is a ransom of the soul. Dynamite
divinizes them, uniting
oneiric sensoria the poem inundates
with vatic thrumming. Thunderclouds
agonize the days the way bison agitate the plains—
plodding, hieratic, animalian, noble.
Eerie flashes of light.

Earth like a sorcerer's secret source.
Earth like a pouch of salt and thyme.
Earth like a frothing mold,
a life form of crushed leaves, an agarical musk
this down-ball funk in a secret air opening slowly inward.

::

unearth
cloud

enearth
clod

enlume
cloud

unlume
earth

skybind
lightning

skywrite
outlease

GREENSHINE

AN ODE

Not when before me the towers of alchemy rose up and I could feel
the tremors of irregular motion between them;
and not when the asp of an anguish sunk its fangs into the soft meat
beneath my thumb; and not when that anguish
transformed into a knowledge you felt some respect for;
and not even when I was lecturing before the learned communities
intent on exploring proximities of sleep and coincidence;
and not even when they began to say my name and gasped at things I was
    saying—

No.
But when I
worked my way through the tedious checkpoints
and I listened to the necessary interrogations
and then wound my way from one kind of ecology to another;
and when I strained forward into the greens of the forest snares of rain
percussed from; and when all of the salt riming the breezes
catalyzed my mental and natural conjunctions,
and when the light so finely filtered in down-drawn drizzle grumed shadow
from moisture, and when the tussocky enclosures
opened before me and the duff was eruptive

and soft as memory foam
and the tufted grasses were stooping under the weight of the rainshine
and the needles of the conifers drew down the dewfall
and the transparency of things lay hidden in attention,
yes—
and then when I started to see
and when the edular earth-domes lacquered with sea-glaze
began to appear, their burnished mahogany
appealing as Hermes' invention of the lyre from the shell of a tortoise,
unearthing them yes and sniffing their reticulated stems a must of spores
    invisibly powdered
and kissing them tenderly
in the lasting largeness revealed in the shining green—yes,
then. And then again. Then and then
was I euphoric.

::

Afterword

1.

The Earth is in *crisis*. Anthropogenic climate change has altered the atmosphere, primarily with the excessive introduction of carbon dioxide, a harmless chemical compound that has typically comprised less than 280 parts-per-million by volume in pre-industrial times—with modulations varying between 180 and 250 parts-per-million over the past 400,000 years—but will menacingly exceed 395 parts-per-million, the present concentration, in the coming years, to continue to spike upward with no indication of slowing down, such that the typically harmless compound will have transformed into a *toxin*, a result of its ability, in such concentration, to increase the atmosphere's radiative properties in reflecting heat back to the Earth.

The evolutionary fact that defines human culture, even more than our ability to digest starches (to which Carl Sauer attributed the success of early human settlements), is that we burn shit to get its energy. Realistically, until this habit changes, we will not stop emitting toxins into the atmosphere. Since the past two hundred years have seen such a dramatic upturn in human population of the planet—from one to seven billion people—and since that accelerated growth depends on the burning of fuels for energy, the likelihood of this changing for the better is remote.

The maxim at the center of Paracelsus's alchemy was *the dose makes the poison*. In other words, an ordinarily harmless substance when overconsumed becomes deadly. We would have done well to abide by this tenet. Alas, humans are impressively adept at creating toxins. Unfortunately, we are inept at destroying them.

2.

Crisis: *chrisis*—discrimination, decision, from *chris-ein*, to decide.

In pathology, a crisis is the point in the progress of a disease when an important development or change takes place which is decisive of recovery or death; the turning-point of a disease for better or worse.

In astrology, a crisis is the name for a conjunction of the planets which determines the issue of a disease or critical point in the course of events.

Toxin: from the medieval Latin, *toxic-us*, poisoned, imbued with poison.

3.

Astrology is an esoteric system, built like alchemy, like Gnosticism, like Kabbalism, from the homo-analogical principle, which is the theory of correspondences that tells us all things, great and small, are linked together. "The Zoharic worldview," Joseph Dan tells us, "is based on the concept of reflection: everything is the reflection of everything else . . . The universe reflects in its structure the divine realms, and events in it, in the past and in the present, parallel the mythological processes of the divine powers."[1]

It's true. The crisis of the Earth is reflected in our politics and government, whose professions are bilious and poisonous. And isn't our poetry just as implicated in this concept of reflection? Isn't poetry also at a crisis point? Isn't poetry also rife with toxins?

4.

from "Poem of the Sayers of the Words of the Earth"

Earth, round, rolling, compact—suns, moons, animals—all these are words,
Watery, vegetable, sauroid, advances—beings, premonitions, lispings of the future—
these are vast words

::

I swear there is no greatness or power that does not emulate those of the earth!
I swear there can be no theory of any account, unless it corroborate the theory of the
earth!
No politics, no religion, behaviour or what not, is of account, unless it compare with
the amplitude of the earth,
Unless it face the exactness, vitality, impartiality, rectitude of the earth.[2]

5.

Fungi are part of the opisthokonts—a group distinct from plants that also includes animals—called the holomycota and the holozoa.

Animals and fungi once had a common ancestor.

Instead of cells, fungi have hyphae, microscopically thin tubules, that spread through soil and rotting matter like cobwebs. A fungal network of weblike cells is a mycelium.

Paul Stamets has written, "I believe that mycelium is the neurological network of nature. Interlacing mosaics of mycelium infuse habitats with information-sharing membranes. These membranes are aware, react to change, and collectively have the long-term health of the host environment in mind."[3]

How? Mycelium eats by absorbing food through hyphal walls, in the form of sugars and amino acids. Whenever food isn't immediately available, mycelium excretes enzymes to break down the matter of its surroundings. Our stomachs do this same thing, but internally rather than externally.

As it eats, mycelium grows. As it grows, it matures and seeks to reproduce. "Mushrooms," writes mycologist Nicholas P. Money, "are fungal sex organs and the most wondrous inventions of the last billion years of evolutionary history on earth."[4] Biologists and mushroom hunters alike refer to mushrooms as the "fruiting bodies" of mycelium.

Mycelium is a saprotroph, a devourer of dead matter. Without decay and the breaking down of dead matter, our ecosystem would cease to function. It would become inert.

Every environment on Earth harbors mycelia. There are six hundred known species in Antarctica, including three recently discovered rotting the wood of Captain Scott's expedition huts from over a century ago. Fungi have been discovered three thousand fathoms below sea level, in the abyssal zone. Mycologists estimate the existence of 1.5 million mushroom species, a mere fraction of which has been described.

Some mushrooms are vibrantly toxic. *Amanita phalloides*, the Death Cap, contains amatoxins and phallotoxins that, when ingested, begin to break down cellular structure, mainly in the liver and for which immediate liver transplant is a treatment. The Poison Pie mushroom contains hebelomic acid, which will give you a nasty stomach ache. *Amanita muscaria*, the legendary fly agaric, contains muscimol and ibotenic acid, toxins that when ingested in controlled amounts are intensely hallucinogenic. R. Gordon Wasson—mycophile, one-time investment banker, and founder of the discipline of ethno-mycology at the Botanical Museum of Harvard University—proposed that the cultus of activity involved in the foraging, preparation, and ingestion of the fly agaric many millennia ago by Central Asian shamans and Vedic priests in the Himalayas is the original root of religion. Even the mighty *boletus edulis*, the King Bolete or porcini, perhaps the most delicious thing on Earth, contains traces of amatoxins.

I have said already, echoing a claim of Stamets's, humans are adept at inventing toxins but inept at eliminating them. Stamets believes that the time has come to enlist fungi as allies in the effort to eliminate toxins because our solo activities are stressing the environmental recycling systems beyond their limits. Stamets believes that "mycelium operates at a level of complexity that exceeds the computational powers of advanced supercomputers." He imagines mycelium as an enormous, intricate communicating intelligence. By enlisting allegiance with mycelium, we can begin to communicate our intentions to come into balance with the natural world we are degrading with the toxins we make. He calls this process mycoremediation.

"Mycoremediation is the use of fungi to degrade or remove toxins from the environment. Fungi are adept as molecular diassemblers, breaking down many recalcitrant, long-chained toxins into simpler, less toxic chemicals."[5] This remediation happens naturally. Mushrooms around Chernobyl, once edible, have become toxic. But Stamets proposes a process of relatively simple inoculation and "myceliation" of toxic zones with benevolent fungal spores, for instance, to clean up ground toxicity, oil spills, and to break down woodlands ruined by fire.

6.

The Mushroom is the Elf of Plants —
At Evening, it is not
At Morning, in a Truffled Hut
It stop opon a Spot

    . . .

'Tis Vegetation's Juggler —
The Germ of Alibi —
Doth like a Bubble antedate
And like a Bubble, hie —

    . . .

Had Nature any supple Face
Or could she one contemn —
Had Nature an Apostate —
That Mushroom — it is Him![6]

7.

The archetype of the mycelium extends to language. In fact, to me, language is the thing that most resembles the communicating properties of mycelium.

I claimed earlier that poetry is rife with toxins. That sounds like a criticism. It's not. In fact, it's as things should be. Like mycelium, poetry processes toxins: poisons in language, poisons in thought, poisons in the imagination. Poetry is the infectious, noxious, gnostic contagion Robert Duncan conceived it to be.

It's also, to apply Gordon Wasson's notions of mushrooms to poetry, the *Somic germ*. Wasson means that it was *amanita muscaria*, the fly agaric, whose cultivation became the mysterious Soma of the Vedas. In the Vedic hymns, Soma is at once a god, the food of the gods, and a liquor. Wasson hypothesized through linguistic and experiential analysis of the verses in the Vedas devoted to Soma that it could really only reasonably be a mushroom that the ancient poets were praising in their hymns. Soma is the euphoric food of the gods and also the source of human euphoria. An object of terror and adoration.

Just so, poetry is the Somic germ of the imagination. Euphoric. Terrible. To be adored.

8.

a sun struck stinkhorn
sticky with flies
thrusts up under
the skirt of an oak[7]

9.

Essential to mycelium's detoxifying properties is its uncultivated wildness. With only a few exceptions, mainly that of *agaricus bisporus*, the Cultivated Mushroom, which is the white buttons that you buy wrapped in plastic at the supermarket (and from which most other common supermarket mushrooms, such as portabellas, are derived), mushrooms cannot be cultivated. They are essentially wild.

John Cage likened the discovery of a wild mushroom to the sounding of a musical note in a performance: something that can't ever be repeated.

For poetry to do its work, it should be uncultivated, wild; or, like a performance.

10. THE EUPHORIA OF THE FORAY

Cage: "[I]deas are to be found in the same way that you find wild mushrooms in the forest, by just looking."[8]

Gordon Wasson, along with classicist Carl Ruck, coined the word *entheogen*, to refer to the inspiring properties of mushrooms. It means *the thing that awakens the god within*. Though the word was devised as a more descriptive, less psychedelically tainted synonym for the word *hallucinogen*, in my experience the word applies beyond the nominative psychoactivity of mushrooms. Instead, it extends into what I would call *ethno-mycological effervescence*.

Ethno-mycology is the human-mycelial interactive network. Effervescence is Emile Durkheim's term for the collective ideal that religion expresses. In *Elementary Forms of the Religious Life*, he writes, "[E]ffervescence

. . . changes the conditions of psychic activity. Vital energies are over-excited, passions more active, sensations stronger; there are even some which are produced only at this moment. A man does not recognize himself; he feels himself transformed and consequently transforms the environment which surrounds him."[9]

Ethnomycological effervescence is the collective ideal of inter-kingdom, human-fungal communication: Mushrooms are treasures hidden in plain sight that you find "by just looking." They arise like ideas. Looking for edible mushrooms is euphoric because when you do it you effervesce: you are transformed and you transform your surroundings. This enables mycopoetics, a fungal-imaginal making.

Mycopoetic euphoria is effervescent foraging: in language, in dictionaries, in ideas, in old poems, in the poems of the future. It is a pursuit of uncultivated wildness at once restorative (because adept at destroying toxins) and entheogenic, awaking divine awarenesses within.

11. TO THE WOODS

"The Dogwood by the Corner road has lost every leaf—its bunches of dry greenish berries hanging straight down from the bare stout twigs as if their peduncles were broken. It has assumed its winter aspect. A Mithridatic look . . . Saw by the path-side beyond the Conant Spring that singular jelly like sort of Mushroom—which I saw last spring while surveying Whites farm—now red globular ¾ inch in diameter, covering the coarse moss by the ruts on the path side with jelly-covered seeds . . ."[10]

Since a crisis is a critical point in the course of events, what should we do?

I suggest an embargo on any new poetry for two years, to allow for sufficient decomposition and toxin transformation.

Also, it should be noted: the foraging way is the visionary way. Consider the example of Blake's poetry, especially his fixation on Milton's *Paradise Lost*. The poem was one hundred thirty years old when Blake was conducting his obsessive refigurings of that poem. What was Blake doing there in Milton? For one thing, he was foraging and finding, transforming and being transformed.

So, what should we do? I say, go to the woods, go to the words.

---

1. Joseph Dan, *Kabbalah: A Very Short Introduction* (Oxford: Oxford University Press, 2004), p. 33.

2. Walt Whitman, *Selected Poetry*, edited by Gary Schmidgall (New York: St. Martin's Press, 2000), pp. 160, 164.

3. Paul Stamets, *Mycelium Running* (Berkeley: Ten Speed Press, 2005), p. 2.

4. Nicholas P. Money, *Mushroom* (Oxford: University of Oxford Press, 2011), p. 1.

5. Stamets, p. 86.

6. Emily Dickinson, poem 1350, *The Poems of Emily Dickinson*, edited by R.W. Franklin (Cambridge: Belknap/Harvard, 1998), p. 520.

7. Tom Pickard, "Stinkhorn," *Hole in the Wall* (Chicago: Flood Editions, 2002), p. 129.

8. John Cage, *Musicage: John Cage Muses on Words, Art, Music*, with Joan Retallack (Middletown, CT: Wesleyan University Press, 1996), p. 90.

9. Emile Durkheim, *Elementary Forms of the Religious Life*, tr. Joseph Ward Swain (New York: Free Press, 1965), p. 469.

10. Henry David Thoreau, October 5, 1851, *A Year in Thoreau's Journal: 1851* (New York: Penguin Classics, 1993), p. 251.

Acknowledgments

Earth Is Best is the second volume in a projected trilogy about modes of consciousness. The first volume, *Phosphorescence of Thought* (Cultural Society, 2013), concerned itself with the evolution of consciousness. *Earth Is Best* addresses altered states of consciousness. The third volume, provisionally entitled *The Hidden Eyes of Things*, will consider through the discipline of astrology the unconscious. *Earth Is Best* takes its title from the opening three words of Pindar's magnificent first Olympian Ode, *ariston men hudor*, "water is best."

Books about mushrooms as well as mushroom field guides, by John Allegro, David Aurora, Nicholas Money, John Ramsbottom, Peter Roberts & Shelley Evans, and Paul Stamets among others, served as constant resources for these poems, but none was more important and no work shaped the imagination of these poems more avidly than R. Gordon Wasson's *Soma: The Divine Mushroom of Immortality*, a work of sublime audacity and unremitting power. It would not be inaccurate to suggest *Earth Is Best* as marginal commentary for Wasson's *magnum opus*.

I should also mention two sets of forays that informed the work of these poems, one set in books, the other in the world. When I began to work on these poems, I committed myself to reading *The Red Book* by Carl Jung. I treated the project like a discipline. It became a meditation. In the same spirit, I began to read through Daniel C. Matt's magisterial translation of the *Zohar*, patterns of whose language began to inform the composition of these poems.

In the world, I lucked into mushroom hunting thanks to Michael Autrey, who shared with me his secret/sacred spot for porcinis, as well as a feeling for when the cosmos is instinctively vibrating at your feet, and to whom therefore this mycopoetic field guide owes its most significant debt.

Some of these poems appeared in the following publications, electronic and print: *The Cultural Society*, *The Dalhousie Review*, *From a Compos/t*, *Hambone*, *Plinth*, *The Poetic Front*, *Reliquiae*, *spacecraftprojects*, and *West Branch*. Many thanks to the editors of these publications. "First Amanita Ode" was published as a broadside by All Along Press in Saint Louis. "Toadstool," in part, appeared in *Nature and Regeneration*, a pamphlet published by Corbel Stone Press. My thanks to Autumn Richardson and Richard Skelton. "Hidden Stone" appeared in *Emerald Tablet*. Thanks to Derek Fenner. Part of "Twenty-Eighth Amanita Ode" appeared in a Winter 2018 digital supplement to *Reliquiae*. Thanks again to Autumn and Richard.

Writing these poems was enabled by two fortunate occasions. The first was a residency at AIR Krems in the summer of 2011, where mushroom forays deep into the Wachovian woods were afforded and where "Hidden Stone" was written. The second was a paid faculty leave from the School of the Art Institute of Chicago in the Spring of 2012, when several of these poems took shape.

Finally, my thanks to Zach Barocas, Devin Johnston, Michael O'Leary, G. C. Waldrep, and Stephen Williams for helping hands. And to Todd Buck for the frontispiece illustration of *amanita muscaria*.

PETER O'LEARY WAS BORN IN 1968 IN
DETROIT, WHERE HE WAS EDUCATED BY
THE LASALLIAN CHRISTIAN BROTHERS.
HE STUDIED LITERATURE AND RELIGION
AT THE UNIVERSITY OF CHICAGO. IN THE
1990S, HE WAS MENTORED BY RONALD
JOHNSON, BECOMING HIS LITERARY EXEC-
UTOR UPON THE POET'S DEATH IN 1998.
IN ADDITION TO DETROIT AND CHICAGO,
HE HAS LIVED IN PORTLAND, OREGON,
ANN ARBOR, MICHIGAN, VIENNA, AND
BUDAPEST. HE IS THE AUTHOR OF FIVE
PREVIOUS BOOKS OF POETRY, NUMEROUS
CHAPBOOKS, AS WELL AS TWO BOOKS OF LIT-
ERARY CRITICISM. HE LIVES IN OAK PARK,
ILLINOIS, AND TEACHES AT THE SCHOOL
OF THE ART INSTITUTE OF CHICAGO AND
AT THE UNIVERSITY OF CHICAGO. WITH
JOHN TIPTON, HE EDITS VERGE BOOKS.